S0-BIJ-017

MASON JAR

JAR

MAGIC

Copyright © 2014 CQ Products
Waverly, IA 50677
All rights reserved.
No part of this book may be reproduced or transmitted in any form or by
any means, electronic or mechanical, including photocopying, recording
or by any information storage and retrieval system, without permission in
writing from the publisher.

Printed in the United States of America
by G&R Publishing Co.

Distributed By:

507 Industrial Street
Waverly, IA 50677

ISBN-13: 978-1-56383-513-1
Item #7111

Treasured...
for more than 150 years!

When John L. Mason invented the mason jar back in 1858, its sole purpose was long-term food storage. In the late 1800s, six Ball brothers began mass-producing glass "fruit" jars and became the leaders in the mason jar industry. And in 1903, Alexander H. Kerr developed wide mouth jars that were easier to fill. Since then, the look of the mason jar hasn't changed much . . .

Until now!

We're pulling the pantry doors wide open to change and reuse mason jars in ways those visionaries never dreamed of!

Displayed on your mantle, perched in your office, or swaying in the breeze from a tree in your front yard, "masons" have tons of potential, and we have big ideas for showing them off.

So come along – we'll show you how to take plain ol' mason jars and give them the renewed purpose they deserve . . . and give *you* something to treasure!

Mason Jars – repurposed, reimagined, reused!

All Shapes, All Sizes...

Mason jars are everywhere, and their variety assures that you have something to choose from when deciding how to use them.

Don't let size fool you – everything has potential. No jar is too small or too large to be filled with inspiration.

Go with the flow. While it generally boils down to personal preference, look for jars with a shape that will best serve your purposes.

Wide Mouth Jars

These jars are great for projects that require placing larger items inside or where the wide opening makes it easier to fill *(for terrariums and cookie mixes)*.

straight jars have very little "shoulder" area

HALF PINT   **PINT**   **QUART**

Look for other shapes and sizes, too.

...Unlimited Uses

They can be painted, embellished, or used for cooking. They go along on picnics. We drink from them and use them to light a path. From wedding décor to gifts galore, filled with cookie mix or candle wax, there's almost nothing mason jars can't do.

And let's not forget the lids! With just a twist and a turn, the flats and rings go from sealing in freshness to baking muffins or crafting garlands, wreaths, and coasters.

Regular Mouth Jars

The opening in these jars is slightly smaller than that of the wide mouth jars. Lids come in a variety of colors and materials; plastic or metal one-piece lids can replace the original two-piece gold or silver ones.

"quilted" jelly jar

plain without logos or other markings

Are you ready to start creating? Let's go!

Picnic Packs

Tuck napkins, straws, and silverware into mason jar "drinking glasses" for grab-and-go entertaining. Change the contents to fit any occasion *(red, white, and blue for a patriotic get-together or bandanas and wooden cutlery for a down-home vibe).*

Hanging Vase

Whether hanging from a shepherd's hook, the backyard clothesline, or your garden gate, this versatile wire hanger lets your mason jars become the star of the show.

1 Leaving a short tail at the start, wrap a long piece of wire around the neck of the jar several times *(below the threads)*, ending where you started; twist the tail and long wire together tightly.

2 Loop the remaining length of wire over the top of the jar to form a handle. Tuck the end of the wire under the wrapped section, bend it up, and twist it around the handle until secure. Clip off any excess wire and pinch well to prevent pokes.

3 Tie a ribbon around the threads of the jar for added decoration. Just add water and flowers and... it's beautiful.

Make several to hang and enjoy.

Mounted Shelf Jars

Mason jars, any size, with
one-piece metal lids

Display shelf

Drill & small drill bit

Screws

Before you begin, decide how many jars will fit under your shelf.

1 Measure and mark the location for each jar lid on the underside of the shelf. **2** Using the drill and bit, make two evenly spaced starter holes through each lid as shown. **3** Attach the lids to the shelf with screws.

Here, yarn passes through a rubber grommet inserted into a hole drilled through a flat lid, $\frac{1}{16}$" to $\frac{1}{8}$" larger than the grommet.

Now simply hang the shelf, fill the jars with little bits of this and that, and fasten the jars to the lids.

To make inserting easy, squeeze the grommet and fit the cut edge of the lid between the grommet's ridges. **Handy dandy!**

Out of the way, but still visible and convenient.

Ring Wreath

- 32 regular-size mason jar rings
- Washi tape (assorted)
- Spray paint
- Medium weight wire
- Plastic disposable lid (slightly smaller than wreath)
- Hot glue gun
- Ribbon

Put it together

Include wrapped, plain, and painted rings in your wreath.

1 Wrap washi tape around the outside of some rings, pressing flat. Leave a few plain and paint others; let dry. **2** Slide all rings, facing the same direction, onto a length of wire. Gather them in a tight circle and twist wire together; bend excess wire into hanging loop and twist securely. Space the rings evenly on wire. **3** Cut out the center of the plastic lid, leaving a ring about 1" wide; glue it to the back of the wreath to stabilize jar rings. **4** Decorate the wreath with ribbon, covering the exposed wire.

Make it patriotic. Use 27 wide mouth jar rings; paint 7 blue, 10 red, and 10 white. Paint 3 wooden stars white. Dry completely. Assemble wreath with wire and ribbon as directed, grouping blue rings together and alternating red and white ones like stripes on a flag. Glue the stars on the blue rings. Add ribbon.

Soap Dispenser

Mason jar, any size, with one-piece metal lid

Drill with 1" hole saw

Soap dispenser pump

Waterproof epoxy

Liquid soap

1 Using the drill and hole saw, make a hole through the center of the lid, large enough for the pump to fit through, but smaller than the "collar" portion *(collar should rest flat on top of the lid).* **2** Trim the plastic pump tube at an angle, if needed, so the tip just touches the bottom of the jar. **3** Apply epoxy *(according to package directions)* along the underside rim of the pump collar and insert the pump through the hole from the top; hold in place until set. Add more epoxy around the hole and the pump on the bottom side; let dry completely. Fill jar with soap and fasten the lid.

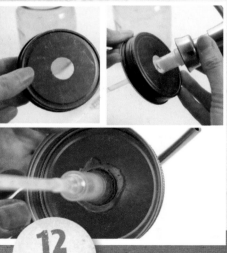

For ease, drill hole with the lid fastened securely to the jar. If available, use a drill press.

Poured Candles

Before you begin, tint mason jars *(we used jelly jars)* and let them dry completely *(see page 24 for directions).*

1 Fill a tin can with blocks of paraffin wax *(old candles would work, too)* and set inside a larger tin can containing about 2" of water. Place on your stove over medium heat to melt the wax. *(Careful – those cans will get HOT!)* **2** Attach one end of a candle wick *(at least 1" longer than the height of the jar)* to a small piece of foil. Pour a little melted wax into the bottom of the jar and set the foil end of the wick into the center; let the wax harden around the foil. When hardened, wrap the other end of the wick around a skewer and set it across the jar opening so the wick stands straight. **3** Slowly pour wax into the jar over the back of a spoon until the jar is nearly full; let the wax harden. If the wax sinks in the center, top it off with more melted wax. Trim the wick, light, and bask in the glow.

Cookies in a Jar

Wide mouth quart mason jar with ring & flat lid

1 tsp. baking soda

½ tsp. baking powder

¼ tsp. salt

1⅔ C. flour

½ C. chopped macadamia nuts

⅔ C. dried cranberries

½ C. white baking chips

⅔ C. brown sugar

⅓ C. sugar

Put it together

Gather a few supplies to make your jar extra pretty. Coordinating paper, ribbon, and a label are all you really need.

1. Stir together the baking soda, baking powder, salt, and flour; carefully pour into the mason jar, level off, and tap down lightly.

2. Layer the remaining ingredients in the order listed, packing each layer gently before adding the next ingredient. Attach the lid.

3. Be sure to give the recipient these mixing and baking instructions along with the cookie mix.

4. Dress it up by adding a label to the front of the jar. Place a paper circle between the flat lid and jar ring and tie on the ribbon. A delicious gift, sure to be enjoyed.

White Chocolate Cranberry Cookies

1 jar cookie mix	1 egg
⅔ C. shortening	1 tsp. vanilla extract

Pour sugar and brown sugar from top of jar into a large bowl. Add shortening; mix at high speed until light and fluffy. Add egg and vanilla; beat at high speed for 1 to 2 minutes. Dump in remaining ingredients from jar and beat at low speed until just combined. Drop dough by tablespoon onto a lightly greased baking sheet. Bake at 375° for 8 to 10 minutes.

Mason Lights

Wide mouth pint or
   quart mason jars
   with rings

Dried beans or filler
   of choice

Votive candles

Drill & small drill bit

1 (15") length chain
   for each jar*

Pliers

* We used #16 chain.

Put it together

Whether you line up these handy lights along a walkway, hang them from the branches of nearby trees, cluster them together on your patio, or scatter them here and there in your back yard, you'll set a just-right mood every time.

1. Fill jars with 1" to 2" of your choice of filler.

2. Push a candle down into the center making sure it's stable.

3. Using the drill and bit, make two small holes on opposite sides at the top edge of jar rings. Attach chain at holes and pinch chain ends closed with pliers.

4. Attach rings to jars, light, hang, and enjoy!

Be creative. These jars can be used in other ways, too. Use marbles for filler, and instead of candles, add flowers and water for a nifty vase.

Use caution. Keep candles away from flammable objects!

Distressed Masons

- Mason jars, any size
- Acrylic craft paint (black)*
- Acrylic craft paint
  (any other color)*

- Foam paint brushes
- 80-grit sandpaper

not enamel or gloss

18

1 Coat the outside of the jars with black paint and let dry. **2** Paint over the black paint with any other color you choose; let dry. See what they look like when they're dry – you may want to give them more than one coat. **3** Dry the final coat of paint overnight.

4 Lightly sand the wording and random other areas where normal wear-and-tear would occur.

Sand off as much or as little as you like to get the look you're after.

Use dimensional fabric paint to make words or designs on a plain mason jar. Draw the lines nice and thick, then don't touch until it's completely dry.

Give the jar a couple coats of acrylic enamel paint, and when it's dry, add some ribbon and fill 'er up.

Mason Jar Cuppies

4 (4 oz.) mason jars with
    white rings & flat lids*

Glue gun

1 (10.1 oz.) tube white
    acrylic latex caulk &
    caulk gun

Seed beads

Cupcake toppers (birthday
    candles, painted
    woodsies, or foam
    shapes)

M&Ms or other small
    candies

* You can paint rings and lids with
    white spray paint and sealer.

Put it together

The frosting on these cute cupcakes never melts! Give these jars as party favors and the recipient can refill them with candy anytime.

1. Fasten each flat lid inside a jar ring with the glue gun.

2. Cut the end off the caulking tube at the thickest part. Then, starting at the center of the lid, squeeze caulk out in a continuous circle, mounding it up as if frosting a cupcake.

3. Sprinkle lightly with beads and add a topper. Let dry completely.

4. Fill jar with candy, fasten lid, and enjoy!

Cupcakes to Go. Set a frosted cupcake on a wide mouth jar lid with ring and set jar over cupcake; fasten jar to lid. Tie on a ribbon and tag, or if your jar is tall, attach the tag to a pick poked into the cupcake before placing it in the jar.

Chalkboard Lids

Mason jars, any size,
   with rings & flat lids

Sandpaper

Spray primer

Chalkboard paint

Chalk

1 Sand and prime the tops of flat lids according to the instructions on the paint can.

2 When the primer is dry, give lids a few light coats of chalkboard paint, letting each coat dry before applying the next one. Dry the final coat of paint overnight.

3 Before you use the lids for the first time, coat the entire painted surface with chalk and then erase with a damp cloth. Fill jars, label with chalk, and attach the lids. Wipe lids with a damp cloth to rewrite anytime.
Presto chango!

Spices, craft supplies, game pieces... endless possibilites.

Rustic Pumpkin

With just a few quick steps, you can turn your mason jar rings into a festive decoration, perfect for autumn.

1. Give both sides of 20 jar rings a light coat of spray primer and then spray with light coats of orange spray paint until you reach the shade and look you want, letting each coat dry before applying the next one. *(Make sure both primer and paint are suitable for metal surfaces.)* Add a coat of clear acrylic sealer to help prevent scuffed paint, if you'd like.

2. When dry, thread the rings *(all facing the same direction)* onto a length of twine or yarn. Gather them in a tight circle and tie the ends of the twine together; space the rings evenly apart.

3. Add cinnamon sticks for a stem and cut leaf shapes from paper and/or burlap. A pumpkin masterpiece, for sure.

Tinted Jars

Mason jars, any size

Warm water

Gel food coloring, any color

Mod Podge gloss
   decoupage finish

These tinted jars get their transparent color from gel food coloring. Make them as subtle or vivid as you like. (Not intended for use with liquids.)

Put it together

Think of the possibilities – the colors you can create are nearly endless! Make jars for every room of the house.

1 Mix 1½ teaspoons warm water with enough food coloring to get a shade you like. *(For paler jars, use up to 1 tablespoon water.)* Stir in 2 tablespoons Mod Podge until blended and "milky." **2** Pour the mixture into a jar, give it a swirl, and turn the jar to "paint" the entire inside. **3** Hold the jar over a bowl so the excess paint runs out. Wipe off the jar's rim and set it upside down on a drainer over paper to catch drips. Let dry overnight *(move the jar several times to prevent a crust from forming on the rim).* **4** Flip the jar upright and let it dry completely. Use a craft knife to cut away any excess dried paint around the opening.

They appear opaque until they're dry. Patience...

Stenciled Jars

- Mason jars, any size
- Items to use as stencils
- Metallic, gloss, or matte spray paint

Put it together

You can use all kinds of household items as stencils. Here are a few ideas.

Rubber Bands. Attach rubber bands to a jar in any pattern. Spray with several light coats of metallic paint.

Doily. Wrap a doily around a jar and attach the edges in back using a small piece of tape. Tuck any loose ends under and into the jar. Spray over the doily with several light coats of paint. *(The doily can be used for additional jars.)*

Stickers. Attach stickers to a jar and spray with several light coats of paint *(be sure to use stickers that can be easily peeled off the glass).*

For all these projects, carefully remove the stencils when the paint is dry and coat with protective spray, if you wish.

Plain jars work best for these projects.

Pie Tarts

6 wide mouth rings
   & flat lids

Aluminum foil

Cooking spray

1 (15 oz.) pkg. refrigerated
   pie crusts (2 crusts)

1 (21 oz.) can fruit
   pie filling (we
   used raspberry)

1 egg, beaten

Coarse sugar

To prep all recipes on this page, wrap the painted side of the flat lids with foil and set them inside jar rings *(foil side up)*. Spritz with cooking spray and set these "tart pans" on a baking sheet.

1 Bring the pie crusts to room temperature as directed on package; unroll one crust and flatten slightly with a rolling pin. Cut six circles *(bottom crusts)* ½" larger on all sides than a jar ring, rerolling scraps as needed. **2** Press each circle into a tart pan, leaving a small overhang. Spoon filling into each crust until nearly full. **3** Unroll and flatten the second crust. Cut six circles *(top crusts)* ¼" larger on all sides than the ring; cut small vent holes. Moisten the edges of the bottom crusts with water and set a top crust over the filling. Pinch together edges of crusts and flute. **4** Brush on some egg and sprinkle with sugar. Bake at 425° for 15 to 20 minutes or until filling is bubbly and crusts are deliciously golden brown.

Serve directly from the tart pans or take them out first.

* Follow directions for Pie Tarts through Step 2 *(cut 16 circles)* and fill with your favorite pumpkin pie filling. Bake at 425° for 15 minutes or until done.

* Pat your favorite graham cracker crust mixture into pans *(number will vary)*. Bake at 375° for 5 minutes; cool. Fill with ready-to-use cheesecake filling.

Mini Herb Garden

Wide mouth pint or
   quart mason jars with
   straight sides

Stainless steel hose clamps
   (2¹³⁄₁₆" – 3¾" size works
   well for these jars)

Screwdriver

Scrap wood

Drill & small drill bit

Display board with hangers

Screws

Pebbles

Potting mix

Herbs

Plant markers

Put it together

1 Place a hose clamp around a jar *(below the threads)* and tighten the clamp's screw to secure the jar. Lay the clamp and jar on scrap wood with the clamp's screw facing you *(this is the front side)*. Keeping the clamp in place, loosen the screw and remove the jar.

2 Make a starter hole through the back of the clamp using the drill and bit. Repeat with remaining clamps. **3** Determine placement of each clamp on the display board; drive a screw through the starter holes into the display board to secure. **4** Add a 1" layer of pebbles to each jar for drainage and fill jars with potting mix; plant herbs. Hang the board and place the jars in the clamps, tightening screws to secure.

Plant markers. Flatten old spoons with a hammer; then write the herb's name with a permanent marker.

Office Supplies. No green thumb? Fill jars with office supplies instead and hang near your desk.

Painted Lids

Here, jars filled with cookie cutters, ice cream cones, cupcake liners, birthday candles, picks, and sprinkles stand ready for a party. The jars contain clutter and the lids make 'em cute.

1. Lightly sand jar rings and the top of flat lids. Then coat with spray primer and let dry.

2. Give the rings and lids a few light coats of spray paint, letting each coat dry before applying the next one.

3. Now just fill the jars and attach the lids and rings.

Also great for office supplies, craft supplies, or any small collection.

Burlap Jars

Express yourself any way you'd like on these burlap-covered jars.

1. Cut burlap to fit around a plain jar, 2¾" taller than jar's height and about 1" longer than its circumference. Spray one side with adhesive and wrap the sticky side snugly around the jar with 2" extending above the top. Overlap the back edges and press the lower edge over the bottom of the jar. Fold the top edge of burlap into a 1" hem, sticky sides together; squeeze tightly. Cuff the top edge.

2. Using rubber stamps and ink, print a word on the burlap.

3. Pull long threads from the extra burlap (about 25") to tie around the jar's neck (or use cord or chain); add a charm, if you'd like. Oh joy!

Luminaries

They're completely portable, and the flame is safe for everyone.

Battery-operated flameless candles (tea lights or votives)

Tinted mason jars, any size, with rings & flat lids*

* Purchase pre-tinted jars or tint your own (see page 24 for directions).

Put it together

Ambiance... you want it? You've got it! Cast a quiet glow anywhere you want it.

1 For each luminary, put together a mason jar lid and a flat ring. Set on a flat surface, inside facing up, and set a candle in the center of each.

2 Turn a mason jar upside-down over it and screw it onto the lid. When you're ready to use it, just unscrew the jar and activate the candle.

<u>**Solar Lights.**</u> For each, put glass rocks in a mason jar. Remove the stake from a small outdoor solar light, and fit the solar portion into a jar ring so solar panel faces up; attach to the jar. Set in the sun to "charge." Then just watch the lights come to life at night.

A bright light is a frightful sight at night! But these are just right.

Garland Rings

Jar rings (1 per letter)

Heavy paper in
  contrasting colors*

Glue

Double-stick tape

Soft tulle, mesh metallic
  netting, ribbon, or raffia

We used glitter papers.

Put it together

Choose a word(s) for your garland. Cut paper circles to fit inside each jar ring. Cut letters from the contrasting paper and attach letters to circles with glue.

1 Place several pieces of tape around the outside edge of each ring. **2** Cut tulle. For our seven letters *(in regular-sized rings)*, we cut tulle about 8' long and 3" wide *(use more or less depending upon your word)*. Leaving a 5" tail, twist tulle and wrap it snugly around the ring, pressing it against the tape to hold; tie a knot at the top. **3** Leaving about 2" of tulle between the rings, wrap the long end of the tulle around the next ring and tie a knot on top. Repeat to attach remaining rings. Trim tulle ends as needed. Insert the paper circles into the rings and hang.

Coasters. Cut circles from thin cork to fit a wide mouth flat lid; decorate with rubber stamps and waterproof inks or markers. Glue cork to lid; set in jar rings.

Food & Drink Totes

Whip up a bunch of these for a picnic and put them in your cooler until you're ready to eat. Then just dump them out on a plate and the dressing is on top.

For layered lettuce success, put your favorite dressing in the bottom of a mason jar followed by hearty vegetables like pea pods or cherry tomatoes. Then add other favorites, leaving room for leafy greens on top.

Great for toting premixed foods like marinated veggie salad, potato salad, or any other favorite picnic food. The single serving size allows everyone to just grab a jar and eat.

Perfect for transporting drinks and using as drinking glasses, too!

Everyone likes an ice-cold drink on a hot day!

A simple tub or tote with sturdy handles is a fun way to chill the beverages and food you've put in mason jars.

Just pack the tub with ice and your filled jars so the contents will stay cold and fresh. And the best part? People can help themselves!

Pine Flower Vases

- Mason Jars, any size
- Dried pinecones
- Needle-nose pliers
- Cutting pliers
- Jute, burlap, and/or leather cords
- Green spray paint
- Hot glue gun

Put it together

Each pinecone will give you several "flowers." Each flower should include only two or three rows of pinecone "petals" so the flower is no more than ¾" thick.

1. With needle-nose pliers, pull out two rows of pinecone pieces around the entire cone to make space for cutting. Use the cutting pliers to snip through the stem for each flower.

2. For braided trim, cut three long pieces of jute *(for a quart jar, use three 3-yard pieces)* and braid together. Wrap the braid around the jar and glue in several places.

3. Cut burlap leaves and spray lightly with paint. Glue leaves and flowers onto the trim.

Or, fit a burlap strip around a jar and fray the long edges; glue ends in place. Wrap leather cords around jars for a different look.

Sometimes the best decorations are as close as your own back yard.

Memory Jar Tags

Mason jars, any size, with rings & flat lids, plus one extra regular-size flat lid for each jar (for tags)

Decorative paper

Double-stick tape

Permanent marker, optional

Jute, twine, ribbon, string, or elastic

Put it together

Paint rings and lids for the tops of jars as desired *(see page 32 for directions)*.

1 Create a paper tag to fit the underside of each painted flat lid that lists special details about that jar's contents; attach with tape *(or use a permanent marker to write the details directly on the underside of lid)*. **2** Now create another paper tag to fit the underside of each extra regular-size flat lid *(leave the rubber rim uncovered to give your tags uniform borders)*. Fasten these paper tags to the lids with tape. **3** Wrap the neck of each jar with jute and attach your lid tag to it with hot glue. **4** Fill your jars and attach the lids.

Make a Bank. Cut heavy decorative paper to fit inside a jar ring; attach with hot glue. Use a craft knife to cut a hole in the center of the paper. Attach and start saving!

A great way to display special memories.

Decoupage Designs

Plain Mason Jars, any size

Leaves

Sponge brush

Mod Podge gloss decoupage finish

Clear acrylic sealer spray

Leather cords or jute

Put it together

Collect pretty leaves, flexible and smooth enough to press flat against a jar. Press leaves between layers of waxed paper overnight – or use silk leaves instead.

1. Brush Mod Podge on the outside of jars. Then spread more on the back of leaves and press onto the jars as flat as possible.

2. Brush Mod Podge generously over leaves and pat all over with the brush for a bumpy stippled look. Continue to press leaf edges flat as Mod Podge dries.

3. When completely dry, spray with acrylic sealer and let dry again. Tie cord or jute around the threads of the jars.

Use Tissue Paper. Cut colorful shapes from tissue paper with punches or scissors and apply with Mod Podge as directed.

Photo Jar

Mason Jar, any size, with any type of lid

Filler of choice

Photos (or copies of them)

Shells or other decorative items

Sharp knife

Champagne or wine cork

Permanent marker

Hot glue

Jute, twine, ribbon, or string

1 Fill the bottom of the jar with any type of filler you'd like *(we used sand to match the theme of the photos we were using)*. **2** Set a photo down into the filler. The filler will hold the picture upright. Add any decorative items you'd like and tighten the lid on the jar. *(The addition of a second photo on the back side makes for a frame that looks great from any angle.)* **3** Cut slices from the cork and use the marker to write letters on those slices to form a word. Tie jute around the jar leaving a long tail and then glue on the letters.

What a great way to display your favorite photos!

Magnetic Frames

Add pizzazz to photos you have on your refrigerator with these adorable frames.

1. Decorate mason jar rings by winding decorative tape or ribbon around them *(or leave them plain)*.

2. Cut photos to fit inside the rings. You can use either of the rings' openings for the frame, just cut photos accordingly. Attach with tape or glue dots.

3. Attach adhesive-backed magnetic tape to the back of your photo *(or use hot glue to attach another flat magnet)*.

<u>Make an ornament.</u> Attach photo inside a jar ring, but omit the magnet. Cut ribbon to fit around the ring, adding 4". Starting at the center of the ribbon, hot glue it around the outside of ring, with ends even on top; knot ends together.

Mason Sippers

Mason jars (or mason jar
  mugs), any size,
  with rings & flat lids

Scrap wood

Drill & drill bit (1/16" larger
  than outside diameter
  of grommets)

Rubber grommets
  (3/8" hole)

Straws

These jars are an excellent choice for picnics. The handcrafted tops keep those pesky bugs at bay while making your drink easily accessible. And it couldn't be easier! Now let's make Mason Sippers!

1 Set flat lids on scrap wood. Using the drill and bit, make a hole in each lid. **2** Carefully fit the grommets into the holes by squeezing and sliding the grommets into place. **3** Fill jars with your favorite beverage, attach lids and rings, add straws, and sip.

Hold onto the lid tightly to drill. Pinched fingers are no fun!

Lazy Sippers

Flatten paper cupcake liners *(regular for regular jars; jumbo for wide mouth)*. Cut a tiny "x" in each liner for straw placement. Fill jars with beverage, set liners on top, and attach jar rings. Don't forget the straws!

Or cut circles from paper to fit inside jar rings; punch a hole in each for a straw. Attach circles and rings to jars and insert straws.

Ombre Jars

Mason jar, any size

Glossy acrylic craft paint, any color

Glossy white acrylic craft paint

Make one of these beach-y beauties to match your home's décor, or make someone else's day by giving it as a gift.

Put it together

1 Pour colored paint into a jar and swirl to coat just the bottom third. Set upright to dry 24 hours *(longer if paint is thick).*

2 For the lighter middle color, mix some white paint with the original color and pour it into the jar. Tip the jar to paint the middle section. Set the jar upright until dry.

3 Add even more white paint to the original color to make an even lighter shade and coat the rest of the glass. This time, turn the jar upside down and set on a drainer over paper to dry several hours and then finish drying upright.

Marbleize. Pour metallic acrylic craft paint into jar; rotate to cover part of the glass with paint. Turn upside down and "steer" paint where you want it. Set on a drainer over paper to dry. Repeat two more times, using different metallic paint each time.

Plain jars work best for these projects. Not for use with liquids.

Terrarium

Large mason jar with ring & flat lid

Small rocks and tiny pebbles

Activated charcoal/carbon

Potting mix

Tiny plants suitable for high humidity

Larger rocks & decorative items

Spray bottle

Put it together

A terrarium is a wonderful way to bring a little nature into your home.

1 Place 1" to 2" of small rocks in the bottom of the jar; add pebbles to fill in the spaces between rocks. Add a 1" layer of charcoal to help keep the air and soil fresh. **2** Mix just a little water with the potting mix until barely damp; add to the jar until ⅓ to ½ full; pat down to remove any air pockets. **3** Remove plants from their pots and pull roots apart gently. Dig small holes in the potting mix for the plants and set plants in the holes; cover roots with potting mix. Add larger rocks and decorative items around the plants. **4** Use the spray bottle to carefully mist the plants with water. Add the ring and lid to seal in moisture, and set in a well-lit area.

Mist with water occasionally as needed to retain moisture in terrarium.

Candy Bouquet

Quart mason jar with ring

Foam (we used a chunk
  of hollow foam pool
  noodle)

Candy bars (regular
  and mini)

Metallic streamers/icicles

Confetti

Bamboo skewers

Glue dots or low-temp
  glue gun

Wide ribbon

Put it together

This bouquet is a perfect one-size-fits-all gift. Sweet!

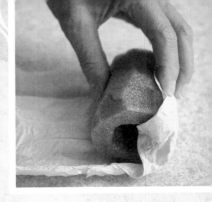

❶ Trim foam to fit inside the jar, short enough to set below the lip of the jar and narrow enough so there's room for candy between the foam and jar. Wrap the foam with tissue paper. ❷ Put some streamers and mini candy bars into the jar, leaving space in the center for the foam. Hang additional streamers over the top edge of jar, if you'd like. ❸ Set foam into the center of the jar and fasten the lid in place to hold streamers. Fill the hole in the foam tube with confetti. ❹ Attach candy bars to skewers with glue. If you'd like, cover exposed skewers with pieces of ribbon. Put candy skewers into center of foam, arranging them as desired and using glue to attach edges together as needed to stabilize. ❺ Tie ribbon into a bow around the jar's rim.

Cocoa Mix Gift

Small mason jars with rings & flat lids

3 C. nonfat dry milk

¾ C. powdered non-dairy creamer

2 C. powdered sugar

2 C. instant chocolate drink mix

1 (3.9 oz.) pkg. chocolate instant pudding mix

1 tsp. salt

1 Combine dry milk, creamer, powdered sugar, drink mix, pudding mix, and salt; stir until well combined.

2 Fill a small mason jar with cocoa mix and tuck it in a basket or bag along with marshmallows and other cocoa-drinking items. Make tags for the jars, if you'd like.

3 Don't forget to include the instructions: Add 4 to 5 tablespoons cocoa mix to a mug and pour in 1 cup of hot milk or water.

Psst: a mason jar makes a great place to store this mix for yourself, too!

Snow Globe

Small mason jar with one-piece lid

Small plastic figurines

Waterproof epoxy

Distilled water

Glycerin

Glitter (not fine-textured)

1 Set the lid on a work surface with the inside facing up and position your figurines on it; turn the jar upside down over the top to make sure the figurines fit into the jar. Remove the jar. **2** Following the package directions, prep the epoxy; apply it to the bottom of the figurines and position them on the lid, holding in place until set. Set aside for 1 hour to cure. **3** Fill jar nearly full with distilled water; add several drops of glycerin and stir. Sprinkle in some glitter and stir again. *(Glycerin keeps the glitter from falling too quickly; if you want to "slow down" the snow further, add a bit more.)* **4** Tip the lid over and carefully lower the figurines into the water. Screw the lid tightly in place, flip the jar over, and give it a shake.

Sewing Kits

Mason jars, any size,
   with rings & flat lids

Scissors

Coordinating paper

Fabric scraps

Fiberfill

Hot glue gun

Cute little sewing kits are great gifts for just about anybody *(maybe even for yourself)*.

① For each kit, use the jar ring as a pattern to cut a circle from the paper and cut a 4" square of fabric. ② For the pincushion, put a small handful of fiberfill on the center of the wrong side of the fabric. Place the top side of the flat lid against the fiberfill, gather the ends of the fabric around the lid, and push the whole thing through the bottom of the ring until the lid presses the fabric against it. Pull on the edges of the fabric until the pincushion looks nice and neat. ③ Glue the fabric to the lid near the outside edges; trim excess fabric. Glue the paper circle over the fabric edges to cover. Fill jars and attach pincushion lids. Poke a few pins into each pincushion and fill the jar with small sewing supplies.

Fill any size mason jar with items to help remind a special friend to take time for herself.

Cut paper to fit inside the jar ring and tie on a fun tag for a memorable gift that she'll be delighted to receive.

59

Breakfast is Served!

Repurpose a cardboard salt box to make a cute sugar and creamer set for your table. Then cook up a yummy breakfast using mason jar rings as cooking utensils.

Put it together

Egg Rounds. Create perfectly round eggs for your English muffins or biscuits. Grease the inside of a wide mouth mason jar ring with cooking spray and set it right side up on a griddle or flat skillet. Heat griddle on medium-low. Whisk eggs in a measuring cup. Holding the ring in place, pour eggs into it, almost to the top. When eggs are set, carefully remove the ring and flip the eggs to finish cooking.

A Pretty Pair. Cut a circle around the pour spout of two empty round cardboard salt boxes to fit inside mason jar rings. Make a "Creamer" and "Sugar" label and attach one to each jar. Fill jars and top with the new spouted lids.

Mason Muffin Pan. No muffin pans in your cupboard? Just set mason jar rings on a cookie sheet and place a cupcake liner in each one. *(Set them upright or upside down, depending which works best with your liners.)* Fill ⅔ full with batter and bake as directed in your recipe.

Microwave Cakes

2 wide mouth 6 oz. mason jars

Cooking spray

6 T. self-rising flour

3 T. brown sugar

1½ tsp. unsweetened cocoa powder

¼ tsp. each ground ginger & cinnamon

Pinch of ground nutmeg & cloves

3 T. molasses

1 egg

Scant 3 T. warm water

Mix 1 egg, ⅛ tsp. salt, ¾ tsp. vanilla, 4½ T. brown sugar, ¾ tsp. baking powder, 6 T. flour, 3 T. each mini chocolate chips, chopped pecans, and melted butter. Microwave in 2 prepped jars* for 80 seconds.

To prep all recipes on this page, spritz wide mouth 6 oz. mason jars with cooking spray.

1 In a bowl, stir together the flour, brown sugar, cocoa powder, and all spices. Add the molasses, egg, and water; stir until well mixed, about 1 minute. **2** Pour half the batter into each jar. **3** Microwave on high for 50 to 60 seconds. Let cool slightly. **4** Garnish and enjoy!

Mix 1 (15.25 oz.) lemon cake mix and 1 (16 oz.) angel food cake mix. In a prepped jar,* stir together 3 T. dry mixture with 2 T. water. Microwave for 60 seconds. Frost. *(Store remaining dry mixture.)*

Grab a fork and serve these right in the jar.

Index